OBOE

BROADWAY FAVORITES

Solos and Band Arrangements
Correlated with Essential Elements Band Method

Arranged by
MICHAEL SWEENEY

Welcome to Essential Elements Broadway Favorites! There are two versions of each selection in this versatile book. The SOLO version appears in the beginning of each student book. The FULL BAND arrangements of each song follows. The supplemental CD recording or PIANO ACCOMPANIMENT BOOK may be used as an accompaniment for solo performance. Use these recordings when playing solos for friends and family.

ISBN 978-0-7935-9842-7

HAL•LEONARD®
CORPORATION
7777 W. BLUEMOUND RD. P.O. BOX 13819 MILWAUKEE, WI 53213

00860036

From Walt Disney's BEAUTY AND THE BEAST: THE BROADWAY MUSICAL

BEAUTY AND THE BEAST

OBOE
Solo

Lyrics by HOWARD ASHMAN
Music by ALAN MENKEN
Arranged by MICHAEL SWEENEY

From the Musical Production ANNIE

TOMORROW

Lyric by MARTIN CHARNIN
Music by CHARLES STROUSE
Arranged by MICHAEL SWEENEY

OBOE
Solo

00860036

From the Musical CABARET
CABARET

OBOE
Solo

Words by **FRED EBB**
Music by **JOHN KANDER**
Arranged by **MICHAEL SWEENEY**

From THE SOUND OF MUSIC
EDELWEISS

OBOE
Solo

Lyrics by OSCAR HAMMERSTEIN II
Music by RICHARD RODGERS
Arranged by MICHAEL SWEENEY

00860036

From EVITA
DON'T CRY FOR ME ARGENTINA

OBOE
Solo

Words by TIM RICE
Music by ANDREW LLOYD WEBBER
Arranged by MICHAEL SWEENEY

Lower notes are optional

MCA Music Publishing

00860036

GET ME TO THE CHURCH ON TIME

Words by ALAN JAY LERNER
Music by FREDERICK LOEWE
Arranged by MICHAEL SWEENEY

OBOE
Solo

From LES MISÉRABLES
I DREAMED A DREAM

Music by CLAUDE-MICHEL SCHÖNBERG
Lyrics by ALAIN BOUBLIL,
JEAN-MARC NATEL and HERBERT KRETZMER

Arranged by MICHAEL SWEENEY

OBOE
Solo

00860036

GO, GO, GO JOSEPH

Music by ANDREW LLOYD WEBBER
Lyrics by TIM RICE
Arranged by MICHAEL SWEENEY

00860036

From CATS
MEMORY

Music by ANDREW LLOYD WEBBER
Text by TREVOR NUNN after T.S. ELIOT
Arranged by MICHAEL SWEENEY

OBOE
Solo

THE PHANTOM OF THE OPERA

OBOE
Solo

Music by ANDREW LLOYD WEBBER
Lyrics by CHARLES HART
Additional Lyrics by RICHARD STILGOE and MIKE BATT
Arranged by MICHAEL SWEENEY

From Meredith Willson's THE MUSIC MAN

SEVENTY-SIX TROMBONES

OBOE
Solo

By MEREDITH WILLSON
Arranged by MICHAEL SWEENEY

From Walt Disney's BEAUTY AND THE BEAST: THE BROADWAY MUSICAL

BEAUTY AND THE BEAST

Lyrics by HOWARD ASHMAN
Music by ALAN MENKEN
Arranged by MICHAEL SWEENEY

OBOE
Band Arrangement

From the Musical Production ANNIE

T-M-RR-W

OBOE
Band Arrangement

Lyric by MARTIN CHARNIN
Music by CHARLES STROUSE
Arranged by MICHAEL SWEENEY

CABARET

Words by FRED EBB
Music by JOHN KANDER
Arranged by MICHAEL SWEENEY

OBOE
Band Arrangement

00860036

From THE SOUND OF MUSIC

EDELWEISS

OBOE
Band Arrangement

Lyrics by OSCAR HAMMERSTEIN II
Music by RICHARD RODGERS
Arranged by MICHAEL SWEENEY

DON'T CRY FOR ME ARGENTINA

OBOE
Band Arrangement

Words by TIM RICE
Music by ANDREW LLOYD WEBBER
Arranged by MICHAEL SWEENEY

From MY FAIR LADY

Get Me to the Church on Time

OBOE
Band Arrangement

Words by ALAN JAY LERNER
Music by FREDERICK LOEWE
Arranged by MICHAEL SWEENEY

I DREAMED A DREAM

OBOE
Band Arrangement

Music by CLAUDE-MICHEL SCHÖNBERG
Lyrics by ALAIN BOUBLIL,
JEAN-MARC NATEL and HERBERT KRETZMER
Arranged by MICHAEL SWEENEY

From JOSEPH AND THE AMAZING TECHNICOLOR DREAMCOAT

Go Go Go Joseph

OBOE
Band Arrangement

Music by **ANDREW LLOYD WEBBER**
Lyrics by **TIM RICE**
Arranged by **MICHAEL SWEENEY**

From CATS
MEMORY

Music by ANDREW LLOYD WEBBER
Text by TREVOR NUNN after T.S. ELIOT
Arranged by MICHAEL SWEENEY

OBOE
Band Arrangement

00860036

From THE PHANTOM OF THE OPERA
THE PHANTOM OF THE OPERA

OBOE
Band Arrangement

Music by ANDREW LLOYD WEBBER
Lyrics by CHARLES HART
Additional Lyrics by RICHARD STILGOE and MIKE BATT
Arranged by MICHAEL SWEENEY

From Meredith Willson's THE MUSIC MAN

SEVENTY-SIX TROMBONES

By MEREDITH WILLSON
Arranged by MICHAEL SWEENEY

OBOE
Band Arrangement

00860036